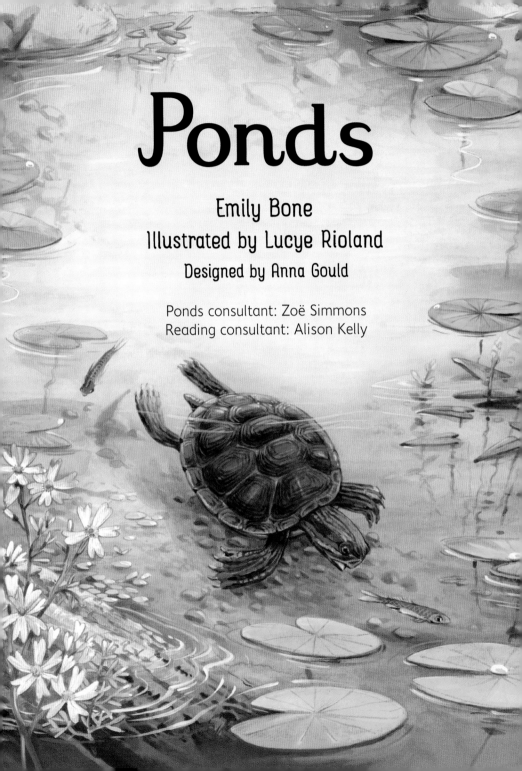

Ponds

Emily Bone

Illustrated by Lucye Rioland

Designed by Anna Gould

Ponds consultant: Zoë Simmons
Reading consultant: Alison Kelly

Contents

Pond life

Lots of different plants and animals live in ponds.

Dragonflies and damselflies fly over the water, hunting for bugs to eat.

Pond plants

Many plants grow in ponds.

Water mint

Water weed grows completely underwater.

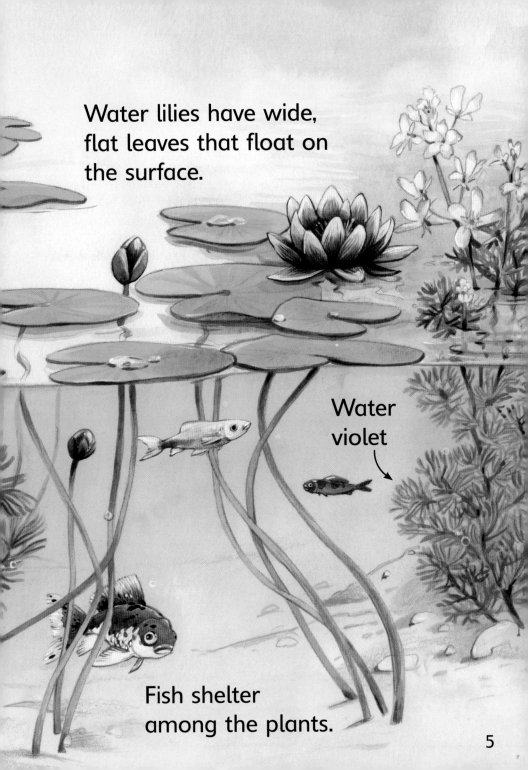

Water lilies have wide,
flat leaves that float on
the surface.

Water
violet

Fish shelter
among the plants.

5

Something fishy

Ponds are home to lots of different fish.

Stickleback fish have spiky fins on their backs. Father sticklebacks look after their babies.

Some goldfish have patterns on their bodies and flowing fins and tails.

Koi carp come from Japan.
They can grow very large.

Underwater hunters

Some pond animals are
fierce hunters.

Great diving beetles swim very
fast. They dive down to catch
fish to eat.

Whirligig beetle

Water scorpions use big pincers to grab food.

Tadpole

Jaw

Young dragonflies, called nymphs, have long, sharp jaws to catch other animals.

Growing up

A dragonfly nymph climbs up a plant.

Nymph

Suddenly, its skin splits. An adult dragonfly climbs out...

...and flies away to find food.

Fast fliers

Dragonflies and damselflies can fly very fast. They dash around looking for bugs.

Hawker dragonfly

This dragonfly is chasing a mayfly.

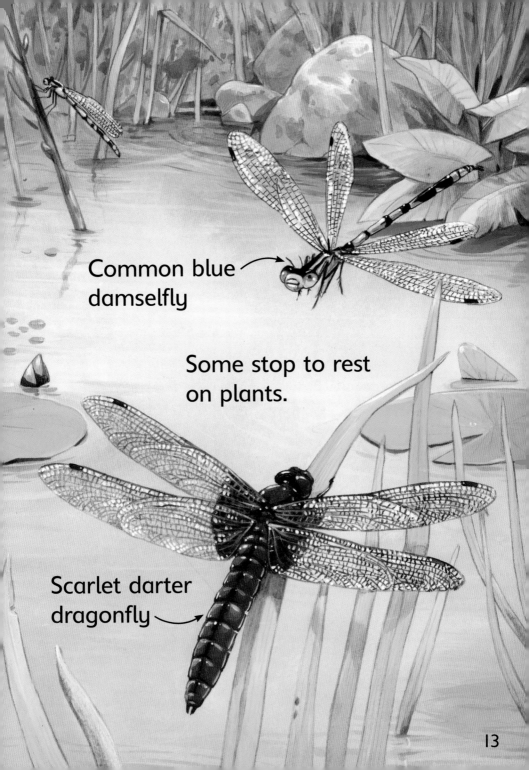

Common blue
damselfly

Some stop to rest
on plants.

Scarlet darter
dragonfly

13

Spring visitors

Frogs, toads and newts come to ponds
in spring to lay eggs.

These are great
crested newts.

They lay tiny
white eggs
on leaves.

Frogs and toads call to find partners.

American
toad

Trill trill trill!

This frog is called a spring peeper.
It makes a peeping call.

Peep peep!

A frog's life

Frogs lay lots of eggs called frogspawn.

Tiny tadpoles hatch out of the eggs.

At first, tadpoles only have tails.
Then, they grow back legs...

...and front legs.
They get bigger too.

Croak!

Finally, their tails disappear
and they turn into frogs.

Pond snails

Pond snails crawl up and down underwater plants.

They have spiky tongues to tear off leaves to eat.

Fish and frogs pick
the snails off the
plants and eat them.

Water spiders

Water spiders live in ponds.

A spider traps air from the surface between hairs on its body.

It dives down and quickly builds a web between pond plants.

It fills the web with the air and climbs
inside. The spider breathes the air.

A young mosquito passes close by.
The spider rushes out to catch it.

Turtles

Turtles lie in the hot sun at edges of ponds to warm up.

They have hard shells.

If there is danger, they can hide away inside their shells.

They slide into the cool water
to hunt for food.

Plop!

Mayflies

Mayflies grow up underwater in ponds.

When they're ready to turn into adults, they come to the surface.

They fly in big groups looking for partners.

Frogs and other animals catch and eat mayflies.

Pond birds

Many different birds live around ponds.

Moorhens build nests and bring up their chicks at the edges of ponds.

Swallows swoop down to snatch bugs
off the surface.

Herons use their sharp beaks to catch
fish from under the water.

Water shrews

Water shrews live in
burrows close to ponds.

They go into ponds
to hunt for fish
and beetles.

A mother water shrew carries a fish
back to her burrow.

She feeds the fish to her babies.

Glossary

Here are some of the words in this book you might not know. This page tells you what they mean.

 fin - thin flap on a fish's body that it uses to move through water.

 pincers - sharp claws some animals have to catch food.

 nymph - the young of a dragonfly and some other animals.

 jaw - part of an animal's mouth.

 newt - animal with a long body and tail that comes to ponds to lay eggs.

 frogspawn - eggs laid by frogs.

 tadpole - the young of a frog.

Frogs have long legs for jumping quickly away from danger.

Websites to visit

You can visit exciting websites to find out more about ponds. For links to sites with video clips and activities, go to the Usborne Quicklinks website at **www.usborne.com/quicklinks** and type in the keywords "**beginners ponds**".

Always ask an adult before using the internet and make sure you follow these basic rules:
1. Never give out personal information, such as your name, address, school or telephone number.
2. If a website asks you to type in your name or email address, check with an adult first.

Index

Acknowledgements

Managing Designer: Zoe Wray

Digital retouching by John Russell

Sun, moon and stars

Farm animals

Elizabeth I

Rubbish & Recycling

Dogs

Horses and ponies

Spiders

Planes

Cats

Ancient Greeks

VOLCANOES

DINOSAURS

Your Body

Armour

Sharks

The Celts

VIKINGS

Castles

How flowers grow

Digging up the past

Caterpillars and Butterflies

Ballet

Pirates

EGYPTIANS

Bats

Eggs and Chicks

ROMANS

Weather

Tadpoles and Frogs

Why do we eat?

Under the Sea

Bears

AZTECS

TRUCKS

Night Animals

Firefighters

Antarctica

Bugs

COWBOYS

Planet Earth

London

Seashore

China

Dangerous Animals

Rainforests

Trees

Reptiles

Ships

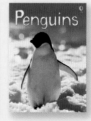
Penguins

The Solar System